Mary Holds My Hand

A Child's Book of Rosary Meditations

by Michele E. Chronister
Illustrated by Heather Sleightholm

This book is dedicated to my dear girls, Therese and Maria. Thank you for teaching me to fall in love with our "Mommy in heaven." May you always know of her (and my) love for you. - Michele

Dedicated with love to my two sweetest blessings: Audrey and Robbie. -Heather

Foreward

In *Rosaries Aren't {Just} for Teething*, I made a resource for woman (especially mothers) to help them reflect on the mysteries of the rosary. But what about a child's perspective on the rosary? What about the unique way that a child teaches us about turning to Mary as *our* mother?

When my oldest was very small, I remember teaching her about Mary. From the beginning, I wanted her to relate to Mary in a very personal way – as her mother in heaven. She already had a deep love for her patron saint (to the point of insisting that she was, "My saint! Nobody else's!"), but we wanted to help her know the Queen of All Saints.

What helped her (and continues to help her) relate to Mary, is referring to her as our "Mommy in heaven." I simply love that. It is simple, but it strikes right to the heart of the matter. Mary was given to us, by Jesus on the cross, to be our heavenly "Mommy." When I attach the word "Mommy" to Mary – a word my children use for me, and a word that I used for my own mother when I was small – I find myself viewing Mary differently. She is our "Mommy." She dotes on us, loves us, showers us with tenderness, and advocates for us constantly. These are the things a Mommy does, because a Mommy loves her little children.

As I've raised my girls, and as a catechist to small children, I've scoured bookstores for good books on the rosary for children. I've found some lovely picture books; books that are excellent visual guides for children to imagine the Mysteries of the Rosary. What is harder to find is a book that has good, age appropriate reflections. It seems that such books are either overly simplified (telling the highlights of the story) or overly complicated (explaining the mystery in more sophisticated language).

What I've written here is a book that I would (and will) use with my daughters. For each mystery there is a very simple, short reflection, written in verse. Since these reflections are geared for pre-readers and early elementary aged children, they are designed to be read aloud, and prayed together with Mom and Dad. I deeply hope that it will help your little ones both to understand the Mysteries of the Rosary, as well as to ignite their little hearts with love for God.

Table of Contents

The
Joyful
Mysteries

The Annunciation

Read aloud: *In the Annunciation, we remember when the angel Gabriel came to Mary, and asked her if she would be the mother of God – the mother of Jesus. She says yes! Let's imagine that we are there, with her, when the angel comes. Close your eyes. Take a few deep breaths. Listen.*

You are busy, Mary.
You are tidying your bed, whispering your prayers.
Your eyes look heavenward, and your heart does, too.
I follow at your feet, like I do with my own Mommy.
You smile down at me, with love.
I am happy to be near you.

Suddenly, a great light fills the room.
I am scared.
It is an angel, greeting you.
Asking you if you will be a mother, a mother to a baby boy.

You say yes.
I don't know why, but I feel joy fill my heart.
Now, Jesus is here.

The Visitation

Read aloud: *In the Visitation, we remember when Mary went to go visit her cousin, Elizabeth. Baby John the Baptist was in Elizabeth's "tummy," and baby Jesus was in Mary's. When Mary says "hello" to Elizabeth, even her baby is happy to hear Mary's voice! Baby John kicks, kicks, and jumps for joy, because he knows Jesus is near. We are happy, too, just like John. Let's imagine that we are with Mary, as she visits her cousin. Close your eyes. Take a few deep breaths. Listen.*

It has been a long, dusty journey.
We are at your cousin's house, Mary.
She smiles to see you, and I smile and wave when I see her.
Her tummy is big and round. I think there is a baby inside!
You shout out your greeting to her.
Suddenly her face changes.

She stops, and she puts her hand on her tummy, and she says the baby is jumping!
She looks surprised, and then her face is full of joy.
She says to you,
"Blessed are you
Among women."

Elizabeth knows. She knows that Jesus is here.
Her baby knows, too.

The Nativity

Read aloud: In the Nativity, we remember the night that baby Jesus was born. He was a tiny, little baby, just like you once were. Even though He is God, He becomes very small, because He loves you. Let's imagine that we are sitting in the stable, beside Mary. Close your eyes. Take a few deep breaths. Listen.

There is a little baby in your arms, Mary.
Jesus is here!
His hands are so small, smaller even than mine.
He grabs my finger, and won't let go.

He lets out a little cry
And you softly hush him.
You rock him
Stroke his feathery hair.
You smile at me, and stroke my hair, too.

I am happy to be here with you, with him.
I lean over and kiss his soft cheek.
Soon the shepherds will come.
But for now, it is quiet.
I look with love at this baby king.

The Presentation in the Temple

Read aloud: *In the Presentation in the Temple, baby Jesus is still very, very small. Mary and Joseph take Him to the Temple. The Temple was like a big church, where they went to pray to God, and to worship Him. Let's imagine that we are at the Temple with them. Close your eyes. Take a few deep breaths. Listen.*

The Temple is so big, and so beautiful.
There are so many people here.
Many of the people are carrying babies, too.
Mary, you carry Jesus.
He is sound asleep
Wrapped in his soft, snowy blanket.

We start climbing the steps.
The steps are big, and Joseph holds my hands
So I won't fall.
We are going to go up and pray.

A man comes.
He looks very old.
He says his name is Simeon
And you let him hold Jesus.

What is that he is saying to you, Mary?
"A sword will pierce your heart?"
What does that mean?
Your smile disappears.
You look very sad.
I slide my hand into yours, Mary, and hold on tight.

The Finding in the Temple

Read aloud: *In the Finding in the Temple, we remember another time that Jesus visits the Temple. This time He is twelve years old, almost all grown up! But this time, Mary and Joseph lose Him. Let's imagine we are looking for Jesus with them. Close your eyes. Take a few deep breaths. Listen.*

Jerusalem is so big.
It is a great, big city.
Jesus is nowhere to be seen.

Just three days ago, he was with us.
I played with him.
We laughed together.
He knew how to make me smile.
But now
Jesus is nowhere to be seen.

I see your face, Mary.
Your eyes shine with tears.
Your face is tired, troubled.
Jesus is nowhere to be seen.

I showed you all the places
Where he and I played.
Round each corner
Inside each crevice
Jesus is nowhere to be seen.

We climb the temple steps.
We are going to pray.

You drop my hand, Mary, when you see him
And you run.
Relief floods your face, as you see Jesus there.
And you hold Jesus tight.
"My son," you say, "Why have you done this?"

He says,
"Didn't you know I must be in my Father's house?"
You ponder these words in your heart.
For now, you are just glad
Jesus has been found.

The Luminous Mysteries

The Baptism in the Jordan

Read aloud: *In the Baptism in the Jordan, we remember when John the Baptist, Jesus's cousin, baptizes Him in the Jordan River. His baptism isn't like ours, because Jesus is without sin. But His baptism makes ours possible. Let's imagine we are standing with Mary, beside the Jordan River, watching. Close your eyes. Take a few deep breaths. Listen.*

The sun is so hot, Mary.
The water looks so cool.
I want to play in it. I want to swim.

You tell me, Mary, that the people are not here to swim.
They are here to be baptized, to tell God they are sorry
For all they have done wrong.
To repent.

I watch as Jesus walks into the water.
I am confused.
He has not done anything wrong!

John, Jesus' cousin and the one who is baptizing
Looks confused, too.
He tries to tell Jesus that he, John, is not worthy to baptize him.
Jesus speaks to him
Reassures him
And John pours the water over Jesus' head.

Suddenly, a loud noise.
It sounds as if someone is speaking
Shouting from heaven itself.

I hear the words,
"This is my beloved Son...
Listen to Him."

I am very quiet.
I look at Jesus
And I listen.

The Wedding Feast at Cana

Read aloud: *In the Wedding Feast at Cana, we remember the very first miracle Jesus did. A miracle is a wonderful, amazing thing. It is so amazing because it is when something happens differently that how it normally happens. In this miracle, Jesus changes water into wine, at Mary's request. Imagine you are following close behind Mary, as she talks to Jesus. Close your eyes. Take a few deep breaths. Listen.*

I cling to your skirts, Mary.
The party is so big
So much dancing, music, and laughter.
I am happy to be here with you.

You are talking to Jesus.
You tell Him,
"They have no more wine."
You don't want the people to have nothing to drink.

Jesus tells you His time
Has not yet come.
And you tell the servants,
"Listen to Him."
And I listen, too.

Such big, big jars they bring!
They fill them with water
To the brim.

Jesus prays over them.
He sends out a pitcher
To be tasted.

It is no longer water!
It has become the very best wine.
You smile, Mary, knowingly.
You knew all along
That Jesus would provide.

The Proclamation of the Kingdom

Read aloud: *In the Proclamation of the Kingdom, we remember when Jesus told everyone the good news of the Gospel, and when He sent out His disciples to spread that good news. Imagine that we are watching Him preach, with Mary. Close your eyes. Take a few deep breaths. Listen.*

We stand beside you, Mary
On this beautiful hillside.
The grass is green, rustling softly in the breeze.
There are people everywhere, and they are listening
Listening to Jesus.

"Blessed are the poor in spirit
For theirs is the Kingdom of Heaven."

"Blessed are the meek
For they shall inherit the Earth."

I want to be meek, poor, and humble, Mary.
I want to be like you.
I want to love Jesus.
I want to love Him, with all my heart.
I want to love Him, like you do.

The Transfiguration

Read aloud: *In the Transfiguration, we remember when Jesus climbed up Mount Tabor, with Peter, James and John by His side. While He was up there, His clothes became dazzling white, and He was joined by Moses and Elijah, coming to visit from heaven. Mary wasn't there when this happened, but we can pretend that we are. Close your eyes. Take a few deep breaths. Listen.*

It is beautiful, up here on the mountain.
We are so high up!
It was a long climb, and my small legs
Are so very tired.

I rest beside your friends, Jesus.
I see you climb higher, to pray.
I know I am safe.
Safe here, with you.

Suddenly, I see
Your clothes have become shining and bright!
There are two men standing with you
Talking with you.
You are all so bright
And I don't know what to say.
Your friends are amazed, too.
We hear a voice,
Loud and deep.
"This is my Son."

Suddenly, the dazzling light dims.
And we are here, again
With only you, dear Jesus.

The Institution of the Eucharist

Read aloud: *In the Institution of the Eucharist, we remember when Jesus ate the Last Supper with His Apostles, the night before He died. At this special, special meal, He gave us the gift of the Eucharist, His Body and Blood. The Bible does not say that Mary was present, but we can pretend that we are, watching quietly. Close your eyes. Take a few deep breaths. Listen.*

You are sitting at the table, Jesus.
Sitting with your friends.
You are eating a meal with them, Jesus.
Eating with your friends.

I am reminded of when I eat with my friends.
But something is different.
There is a sadness here
A sadness I don't understand.

Suddenly, I see you take the bread.
You say words
Words that I have heard before.
"Take and eat, this is my Body."

I see you take the cup.
You say words
Words that I have heard before.
"Take and drink, this is my Blood."

With these words I know
That you will always be with me.

These are the words I hear at Mass.

No longer bread
But Your Body.
No longer wine
But Your Blood.

Quietly you wait each day
Wait inside my church.
You wait for me.
You wait inside the tabernacle.
You want me to know that
I am never alone.

The
Sorrowful
Mysteries

The Agony in the Garden

Read aloud: *In the Agony in the Garden, we remember Jesus' great sorrow, as He prayed in the Garden of Gethsemane. His friends, the Apostles, came with Him. Jesus asked them to stay awake with Him, but they fell asleep. Jesus is praying all alone, and He is very sad. When He is finished praying, the soldiers come, and take Him away. We can pretend that we are in the Garden, too, there with Jesus and the Apostles. Close your eyes. Take a few deep breaths. Listen.*

It is so dark here and
You seem so sad, my Jesus.
Suddenly, I am sad, too,
Here in the Garden with you.

You turn to your friends and say
"Won't you stay awake
for just a little while?"
Here in the Garden with you.

You go off aways
I hear you pray,
"Let this cup pass me by."
I wish there was something I could say
Here in the Garden with you.

I feel so sad
Your friends do, too.
We close our eyes, but for a moment
Here in the Garden with you.

Suddenly, you're there again

Your face so tired and weary.
You ask us all, so soft and sad
If we could not stay awake, but a little while,
Here in the Garden with you.

The silence breaks.
There are shouts and noises.
The soldiers grab you, take you away.
I am all alone.
Here in the Garden without you.

The Scourging at the Pillar

Read aloud: *In the Scourging at the Pillar, we remember when the soldiers were very, very mean to Jesus. The tied Him up, and they hit Him many, many times. It makes us sad when we see Jesus hurting like this. We can pretend that we are quietly holding Mary's hand, trying to comfort her as this happens. Maybe she is comforting us, too. Close your eyes. Take a few deep breaths. Listen.*

It is morning now.
The night was very long
So very dark.
I hold your hand, Mary,
As we look for Jesus.

We see Him there
Tied up so tight.
The soldiers go to hit Him
He cries out in pain.
You cry out, too, Mary.

I squeeze your hand.
I try to be so brave
But I am scared
So very scared.

Before I know it
I've begun to cry.
I do not like to see Jesus
So hurt
So pained.

I feel your arms,
Dear Mary.
They wrap around me
And silently
We cry together.

The Crowning with Thorns

Read aloud: *In the Crowning with Thorns, we remember when the soldiers made fun of Jesus. Jesus is the King of Kings, but the soldiers made Him a crown of sharp thorns, instead of a crown of gold. They did not believe He was a king, and so they made this painful crown for Him, instead. We can pretend that we are watching them putting this crown on Him, and showing them to the crowds. Close your eyes. Take a few deep breaths. Listen.*

There He stands.
"Behold, the man."
Jesus stands on the steps
All alone.

He wears a crown
Around His head.
Is it made of gold?
No.
Is it made of silver.
No.
It is made of thorns.
They stick out, so sharp, so pointy.

The crowd begins to laugh.
Mary's eyes fill
Fill with tears.
Her Son is King
But is treated as no King should be.

The crowd yells
Louder and louder they yell.
"Crucify him! Crucify him!"

"Crucify your king?"
"We have no king but Ceasar!"

I do not know who Ceasar is.
But this I know:
That Jesus is *my* King.

The Carrying of the Cross

Read aloud: *In the Carrying of the Cross, we remember when Jesus carried His big, heavy cross through the streets of Jerusalem. While He was carrying it, He fell from time to time. He was very weak. Mary was there, and in the Stations of the Cross, we remember how she went to comfort Jesus. We can pretend that we are with her, comforting Him, too. Close your eyes. Take a few deep breaths. Listen.*

I've seen pictures of the cross,
But I did not know it was
So heavy
So big.
Jesus can barely lift it.

I walk beside you, Mary.
I hold your hand
The crowd presses close
On every side.

We see Jesus fall
Once
Twice
Three times.
At one point, Mary
We are so close.
You reach out, and touch
You stroke His tired face.
You stroke Him with love,
Like a Mother does.

I reach out, too.
I stroke His hand.
I hold it for a moment.
I kiss it.

My kiss is small and
So am I.
But my love for you
Is great.

The Crucifixion

Read aloud: *In the Crucifixion, we remember when Jesus died on the cross. The soldiers nailed Him to the cross with sharp nails that hurt His hands and feet. While He was dying on the cross, Mary and the Apostle John stood there with Him. It was there that Jesus gave us Mary to us, to be our Mother, too. It was there that Mary became the Mother of the Church. We can pretend we are standing right beside Mary as this happens. Close your eyes. Take a few deep breaths. Listen.*

Jesus, you are so high.
I look up, up, up.
I watched as they raised the cross
Up, up, up.

I feel so small, so scared.
I stand beside Mary and
I hold her hand.

I look up to you, dear Jesus
Up, up, up.
I look up at you, with scared eyes.
Up, up, up.

You look down
At Mary
At John
At all those at your feet.
You look down, with love.

What's that you say?
"Behold your mother."

In that terrible moment, you give me a gift.
Mary is now my mother, too.

You bow your head.
You breathe your last.
And suddenly
All is silent.

The Glorious Mysteries

The Resurrection

Read aloud: *In the Resurrection, we remember when Jesus rose from the dead on the third day. On Easter Sunday, the women went to the tomb and they found it empty, with an angel there! The angel told them that Jesus was not dead, but risen! How happy Mary must have been as she heard this. We can pretend that we are with her when she hears this good news. Close your eyes. Take a few deep breaths. Listen.*

The morning is still.
So still, and so quiet.
The sun is just beginning to rise
And darkness is being scattered by the light.

I walk beside you, Mary,
My Mother.
Now I can call you
My Mother.
I am grateful for that gift.

We walk in the early morning
Walk to meet the Apostles.
Quite suddenly
The whole earth shakes.
I cling tighter to your hand.

A few minutes later
A woman comes running.
It is one of Jesus' friends.
She is shouting something.
What is she saying?

"Risen! He is risen!"
Empty is the tomb.
And Jesus lives
Again.

The Ascension

Read aloud: *In the Ascension, Jesus goes back up into heaven, body and soul. The gates of heaven are open now! Because of Jesus' death and resurrection, we can go to heaven, too. Imagine that we are standing on the hillside with Mary, as we watch Jesus going up into the sky, out of our sight. Close your eyes. Take a few deep breaths. Listen.*

The sun is shining.
The wind is blowing.
The clouds are drifting
And Jesus is speaking.

What is it that He says?
"Go out to all the world..."
He is sending us
You and me.

The wind is whispering
As He raises His hands,
Those same hands He raised
On the cross.

The wind is whispering
As He lifts up His eyes
Gazing toward heaven.
You squeeze my hand, Mary.

The wind is whispering
As Jesus begins to ascend

Up and up and up
He goes.

The wind is whispering
As Jesus is hidden from our sight.
All that remains
Is to gaze up, still seeking Him.

This wind is whispering
As an angel appears
And says,
"One day...He will come again."

Pentecost

Read aloud: *In the mystery of Pentecost, we remember when the Holy Spirit came to the Apostles in the Upper Room. Mary was with them. She was the first to receive the gift of the Holy Spirit, at the Annunciation (when the Holy Spirit came upon her and she became Jesus' Mommy). She is here, again, among the Apostles as they, too, are filled with the Holy Spirit. The Holy Spirit comes to them, appearing in wind and tongues of fire. It must have been amazing! We can pretend we are sitting right beside Mary. Close your eyes. Take a few deep breaths. Listen.*

The room is so big and so high up!
I sit beside you, Mary.
The Apostles are around us, so scared,
And I sit beside you, Mary.

Everything is different now,
Different with Jesus gone.
You whisper to me, "He will still provide."
And I sit beside you, Mary.

A loud noise fills the room
A wind, a driving wind.
Fire! I see fire!
Tongues of flame, fill the room.
They rest on the heads of Jesus friends
But their heads do not burn.
Suddenly, they speak, in words I do not know.
Peter rushes from the room.

The Apostles follow.

They rush out to the rooftop.
They speak in words I do not know
But the people below are amazed.

I do not know these words
But these people do.
They understand these words
As if they were their own.

Many are baptized that day and
Something new
Begins.
The Church is born.

The Assumption

Read aloud: *In the Assumption of Mary, Mary is taken up into heaven, body and soul. We don't know who was there when this happened, but we can pretend that we are there, watching as Mary goes up to heaven, to be reunited with Jesus. Close your eyes. Take a few deep breaths. Listen.*

You tell me, Mama
That you are going home.
You smile at me, Mama
For you are going home.

Home to your Son
Whom you love and miss.
Home to the heaven
Where your heart belongs.

I will miss you, my Mother.
I will miss your hand
Holding mine so tight.
My hand so small and safe in yours.
I will miss your arms around me
Comforting me when
I am afraid.
I feel so safe with you.

I begin to cry
My sweet Mother.
You wipe my tears
And tell me not to weep.

"I will always pray for you
My little child,"
You tell me with a smile.
Your gentle eyes look on me with love.

"And one day,"
You whisper,
Gentler still,
"One day you will be home, too."

The Coronation

Read aloud: *In the Coronation of Mary, we remember Mary being crowned Queen of Heaven and Earth. She is the mother of Jesus, the "Queen Mother." She holds a very, very important place in heaven, and in the Church, yet she still looks at us as her little children. She is our "Mommy in heaven." Imagine that we are with her in heaven, seeing her be crowned by her Son. Close your eyes. Take a few deep breaths. Listen.*

I imagine I was there,
Sweet Mother,
To see you crowned
As queen.

You Son looks on you
With pure joy.
He holds in His hand
A crown of gold.

The light is dazzling.
All is at peace.
You bow your head
As you did when first you gave   your "yes."

The angels sing out
The saints rejoice.
The Father says, "Well done, my good and faithful servant."
Finally, you are home.

*A Study of Botticelli's Madonna of the Book

Salve Regina

For the parents: The Salve Regina is a very old, very beautiful hymn to our heavenly Mother. It is usually prayed at the end of the rosary. It can be said or sung (some beautiful sung versions can be found online). Your children will not understand every word, but there is true value in just exposing them to something so beautiful. God works through what is beautiful and good, and He is surely at work in their little hearts.

Hail, Holy Queen, Mother of Mercy.
Hail, our Life, our Sweetness, and our Hope.
To thee do we cry, poor banished children of Eve.
To thee do we send up our sighs, mourning and weeping in this valley of tears.
Turn then, most gracious advocate, thy eyes of mercy toward us.
And after this, our exile, show unto us the blessed fruit of thy womb, Jesus.
O Clement, O Loving, O Sweet Virgin Mary:
Pray for us, O Holy Mother of God,
That we may be made worthy of the promises of Christ.

Printed in Great Britain
by Amazon